THE PATH TO YOUR PEAK

Six Days to Fulfilling

your Personal Potential

By Lazer Brody

A Brody Health and Wellness Publication

D1400737

The Path to Your Peak

TABLE OF CONTENTS

INTRODUCTION

L ife is like climbing a mountain. We stand at the bottom and dream of being on the top. We imagine how exhilarating the view is from the peak. We can see the whole world, as if all of creation is at our fingertips. The air up there is the freshest and most invigorating on earth. Our hearts soar like an eagle.

We all dream of reaching our own peak. There's just one slight nagging detail. How do we get there?

The answer is surprisingly simple and straightforward. You'll find it in the pages of this book.

We all have the potential of reaching the top. People fail to reach their own special peak because of two main reasons: first, they don't properly utilize and take advantage of their personal potential. Second, they don't have a plan. To do anything successfully, whether it's becoming a champion athlete, a successful businessperson, an honor student, an efficient homemaker or anything else you desire to do, you need a *plan*. With that in mind, this book will provide you with a tailor-made six-day plan for success.

This modest but life-changing book is therefore titled, "The Path to Your Peak", and subtitled, "Six Days to Fulfilling your Personal Potential."

As we've said, we all want to reach the top of our own particular field of endeavor. For some, reaching the peak is accomplishing a goal that they never dreamed of accomplishing, like losing fifty pounds or ridding themselves of a bad habit. For others, it's simply gratification and happiness. At any rate, once we learn how to think positively, we already envision ourselves at the top. All that remains are the "minor" technical details of how to get there. But if we don't focus on our goal at the outset, we'll never attain it.

If you didn't yet have a plan to achieve your own special goal, with this book, you now have one that is uncomplicated and straightforward with no fads and thrills. The information in this book is essentially centuries old, based on the ideas of some of the world's greatest minds, but presented in a simple and comprehensible format, which you'll hopefully find reader-friendly.

Here's our plan: this book contains six chapters, or "days". Each day focuses on a concept that is a necessary tool for success. On Day One, we'll get to know ourselves and we'll learn how positive thinking is not merely rosy optimism, but a basic human right. On Day Two, we'll learn how to "navigate" our lives, which means how to determine where we are in life, where we'd like to go, and how to get there. On Day Three, we'll discover how to choose the right path to reach our destination. On Day Four, we'll deal with the pain and gain in our efforts to reach our objective, and how to remain focused on our goal. On Day Five, we'll learn how to deal with setbacks, which are an integral part of any journey to the top. And finally, on Day Six, we learn how to make a second effort, which is the secret to both personal rejuvenation and long-term success.

Dear reader, you're about to embark on an exciting new journey; you'll not only learn how to fulfill your personal potential, but how to maximize it as well. You're also about to meet someone whom you really never knew before – you! That's right; most people are so busy on the chinchilla wheel of rat-race survival that they never get to know themselves. Worse than that, they don't even have the time to look at the color of the sky.

We're ready to start climbing. From this moment on, you're no longer alone. You'll be a big winner too. If you're dubious, then turn the page and read on.

DAY ONE

THE TRUE YOU – THE RIGHT TO THINK POSITIVELY

A successful salesperson believes in the product that he or she is selling. Success frequently eludes people because they don't believe in themselves. And, if you don't believe in yourself, it's a sign that either you don't know yourself at all, or that the image you have of yourself is not at all accurate. This chapter will change all that.

We all want to climb our own personal mountain. We all want to successfully meet life's challenges and end up in the winner's circle. We all want to get to the top.

The first thing we must now probe before

setting out our journey to reach life's peak is something very basic - who am I?

That may seem odd. A person reacts with impatience, "What a silly question! Are you implying that I don't know who I am?"

Unfortunately, modern society, advertising, the media, peer pressure and one's desire or perceived need to gain the approval of others motivate people to play false roles and build facades of false identities. They lose focus of their true identity and genuine individuality. They become confused. A big gap develops between who they *really* are and who they *think* they are. Such "actors" are never happy, and even if they succeed, their success is short-term at best.

People with delusions of grandeur think they're better than they really are. They're frustrated, for they have expectations that they can't ever succeed in meeting. For example, if a person thinks he's a cheetah, he's doomed to frustration. Even if he becomes the fastest human on earth and succeeds in running the 100-meter dash in 9.8 seconds, he'll still be slower than a cheetah.

At the opposite end are the people with inferiority complexes or low self-esteem. They perceive that they lack the tools of success when they really do have the wherewithal to succeed. These folks are the lions who look in the mirror and see a pussycat.

The common denominator of both of the above all-too-common prototypes is that they don't know themselves. They too are play-actors who live in a fantasy world, for neither is in touch with the truth and reality of themselves and their own true aptitudes and abilities.

The moment you decide to look objectively at who you really are and accept yourself for what you are, you take the first wonderful step up life's mountain. The reward is tremendous, for as soon as you get to know yourself and accept yourself for what you are, you gain emotional freedom. Emotional freedom is one of life's greatest gifts, for the emotionally-liberated individual is not emotionally dependent on any other human on earth. The emotionally-free person doesn't need compliments or other "emotional handouts" from other people to feel good about him/herself.

Three Canine Comrades

The following parable will provide you with some insight about what it means to be yourself:

Three dogs were hiking separately up in the mountains. Sudden high winds and a dangerous blizzard threatened their chances of safely returning home. Simultaneously, they reached a clearing. It was a bitterly cold day with poor visibility. The first dog, renowned for his compassion and dedication in helping others, was a Saint Bernard with a small keg of rum around his neck. He said to the other two, "Greetings, my friends! You look very cold. Come have a sip of my rum. It will warm and replenish you. If you're still cold, you can cuddle up to me - my fur is very thick and warm. Please feel free."

The second dog, a Labrador Retriever and a trained guide dog with a wonderful disposition, profusely thanked the Saint Bernard for his kind offer. He then said, "Comrades, I implore you to stick with me.

Between the flurrying snow and the mountain fog, one can barely see. It's easy to become disoriented and to lose direction. I have a very enhanced sense of direction. It's my job to guide others, especially those who can't see. Stay with me and be safe."

After the Saint Bernard and the Labrador Retriever introduced themselves, they turned to the third dog and asked, "Who are you, brother?"

The third dog appeared to be affronted by the two canine comrades calling him brother. He thought to himself, "Can't they see my Grizzly Bear coat? Aren't they afraid that I'll pounce on them?" The Grizzly Bear costume was a little big on him, for he was only a domestic foxhound. But at $24.99 and alterations included, he couldn't pass up the deal. He cleared his throat and tried to growl like a Grizzly. Needless to say, the growl was nothing more than a weird bark. A hound simply cannot speak with a bear's accent.

The two other dogs smiled patiently. Both of them were larger than the grizzly-hound and stronger too. They knew who they were so they didn't have to flaunt their strength. They were quietly confident and certainly not intimidated. "Who are *you*?" they asked.

"My great-grandfather was king of this mountain and my grandfather was the best hunter in this region..."

The Saint Bernard and the Labrador Retriever flashed a puzzled look at one another and then asked the hound once more, "We didn't ask about your ancestors; we asked about you! Who are *you*?"

"Can't you see that I'm a Grizzly Bear?" Again, he tried to growl, but it only made his throat raspy.

The two other dogs once again smiled patiently. Laughing at others was something they would never do. One cannot be happy by treading on others, even if - unfortunately - they do silly things.

The Labrador put his paw gently on the hound's shoulder and said: "Dear canine cousin, your attempt at being something other than yourself is a double tragedy. No matter how hard you try, you'll never be a Grizzly Bear. And while trying to be a Grizzly Bear, you won't succeed at being yourself."

The hound blushed. The Labrador made a lot of sense. He noticed that while he was trying to impress them with his pitiful attempt at growling, they didn't even bark. When you know who you are, you don't have to make noise and other extraordinary efforts to call attention to yourself.

The Saint Bernard, with a canny insight as to the needs of others, said in a kind voice, "Hounds are terrific dogs. They have an excellent sense of smell and are highly loyal. Many countries use them in crime and terror prevention. At airports and borders, they can sniff out explosives, narcotics and other illegal contraband. You don't need that costume, dear Foxhound friend. You have the capability of being great in your own way. Simply be yourself and know who you are. There's certainly plenty to like about you, the real *you*."

The Foxhound never heard such encouraging words. He was always envious of the lions, tigers and bears. No one ever named a professional baseball or football team, "The

Hounds". He never saw a hound in a prestigious magazine advertisement. But that's all fantasizing. On the other hand, the Labrador Retriever and the Saint Bernard knew how to function under extreme conditions. Hardships did not scare them. The Foxhound envied them, for they were wonderful role-models in the real world, especially when conditions aren't always ideal.

He took their advice. He told himself over and over again, "I'm a Foxhound. I too am worthy. I was created with my own talents and abilities. I have a phenomenal sense of smell..."

The three dogs trudged through the snow, braving their way on the icy mountain path while the gusts of wind and snow lashed at them like a frozen whip. Thanks to the Saint Bernard, they could warm themselves from time to time. By virtue of the Labrador retriever - the superb guide dog - they found their way even though they could barely see. And thanks to the Foxhound, who was finally acting as himself, they found food that saved them from starving. Together, they safely reached their destination.

For you to reach your destination, you must know who you are, too.

Body, Soul, or Both?

So, who are we? What are we? You'd be amazed at how many billions of people go through their entire lives without ever asking themselves this critical question.

As we saw in the above parable, the Saint Bernard and the Labrador Retriever could thrive and succeed under the most trying conditions because they knew exactly who they were. Once the Foxhound shed his silly costume and began acting like himself, he too became successful. So, who are *we*?

Modern society and the media tell us that we're a body, a physical entity that thrives on physical amenities and bodily gratification. Such an outlook is a formula for depression and disappointment, for two reasons:

First, if all we are is a body, life becomes hopeless and purposeless, for our physical lives are sorely finite. At the tender young age of thirty, we reach our physical prime. From then on, the body begins a gradual process of degeneration. Every new year brings a pain in a joint, a new wrinkle, or stronger reading glasses. Every day is simply a day closer to the grave. Is that all we have to look forward to?

The second reason that a bodily-focused outlook never succeeds in bringing us true gratification and fulfillment is because we're not mere bodies! Even if we'd succeed in attaining all the physical pleasures we ever dreamed of, we'd still not be happy, for we have needs beyond those of the body. These are our emotional and spiritual needs.

Our emotions come from the soul. The soul is the life-force, the tiny spiritual microchip in our brain that differentiates between a living person and a deceased one. The soul is a tiny spark of Godliness.

A tiny spark of Godliness? That's the good news!

Since the soul is a tiny spark of Godliness, it has the same characteristics that its Creator has. Just as the Creator is infinite, so is the soul. They both defy time and space, and neither ever dies. So, the more we live a spiritually-oriented life, the more we overcome the downward tendency of bodily-oriented depression and disappointment. The soul never gets old. If cared for properly, it never degenerates. And, if we provide its needs, we attain both happiness and inner peace for posterity.

Some people go to the opposite extreme. They become ascetics. They might go to some monastery or forest retreat, starve themselves and meditate. But ultimately, the ascetics become just as frustrated as the bodily-oriented folks. Why? The Creator designed the body as the housing for the soul. True happiness and inner peace depend on a harmonious relationship between body and soul. Therefore, a person must do his or her utmost to maintain the good health of both.

The real "me" is the happy medium between body and soul, when the body's needs are met but when it is subservient to the soul. In other words, the body caters to the soul and not vice-versa. The healthy soul rules out any bodily gratification that is detrimental to the soul, or even detrimental to the body for that matter. For example, as much as the body would like to eat pizza and drink cola frequently, the soul should not allow it to, for it's not healthy. A healthy soul won't let its body indulge in an extramarital relationship either, for such an indulgence – as gratifying to the body as it might seem – is devastating to the soul.

Since the real "you" is the soul that is housed in your body – and not your body alone, then your personal potential is not limited by the body; it's limited by the soul. But, since your soul is a tiny spark of the Creator, and the infinite Creator defies any limitations, then your potential is virtually *unlimited*!

Ask any marathon runner if he or she is capable of running 26 miles (42 km) on bodily prowess alone. They'll all say an emphatic "no". For many years, I engaged in daily long-distance running. My body was capable of running no more than 10 miles, or less than a half-marathon. Beyond that, my running was all "heart", desire and willpower. When the body kicked out, the soul kicked in, for desire and willpower are powers of the soul. This small yet profound example shows how utilization of soul-power and spiritual strength can exponentially expand your personal potential.

This is your task for Day One, dear reader. Realize that you are not just a body. Your new hairdo, your new suit and those six-pack abs that you spend so much time in the gym trying to obtain are just outer embellishments of the real "you". Get to know your soul and its needs. Don't let the body boss you around. Sure, the body must be healthy. Maintaining physical fitness, personal hygiene and a wholesome appearance are matters of basic self-respect. But catering to our bodies alone will not get us to our peak.

As in a marathon, if we're climbing a difficult mountain, our bodies will give up long before we reach the top. But since we've decided that we're going to reach the peak, we'll have to tap into our soul's potential and that personal reservoir of unlimited ability. How do we do this?

By our faith in the all-powerful and omniscient Creator and the awareness that our souls are a tiny spark of Him, we resemble an oil-well that's tapped in to an unlimited underground reservoir of oil. As long as we keep pumping, the black gold continues gushing to the surface. This power of faith, which in Hebrew we call **emuna**, is the greatest potential enhancer in all of creation. It brings our latent, untapped potential gushing to the surface. It enables us to believe in ourselves. It enables us to break the barriers of any limitations that we thought we were subject to.

Our mention of the Creator and faith has nothing to do with religion. Not all "religious" people have faith, and vice versa. Since the Creator defies limitations and is all-powerful, the more we connect with the Creator, the more we expand our potential. It's as simple as that. What's more, the stronger our connection with the Creator, the stronger our souls become. The stronger our souls, the greater our potential. So how do we create a strong connection to the Creator? We speak to Him, in our own language and in our own words. We ask for His help in everything we do. And with His help, we'll make it to the top – wait and see.

The Right to Think Positively

As soon as we understand the rationale of creation, we can begin to think positively. Positive thinking is not some artificial pair of rose-colored glasses; it's a basic human right. Here's how:

A rational individual isn't prepared to do anything that doesn't serve a purpose. For example, if you ask someone to raise and lower their hand for sixty minutes for no apparent reason, they'll certainly refuse. Even if you offer them a fair hourly wage to fulfill your request, they still might not consent if they don't see a purpose to what they're doing.

If a human does things for a purpose only, it goes without saying that the omniscient Creator does nothing without a specific and very good purpose.

Did the Creator create such a magnificent universe – from the tiniest one-celled amoeba to the greatest galaxies – out of boredom? Of course not! Every mineral, plant, animal, and human have an important task to perform in the overall scheme of creation. The Creator instills in every human fabulously sophisticated components - intellectual potential, physical capabilities and spiritual power – for a definite purpose.

Each individual is a part of a greater whole, the whole of creation. Since the whole of creation has a purpose, then each individual has a purpose as well, for each part shares the characteristics of the whole. Do you realize what that means? If the Creator put you here on earth, it means that at this point in time, the world cannot exist without you, for you have your own special purpose on earth. With that in mind, you can believe in yourself, for the Creator has given you your own unique tools to succeed in your own special mission on earth. Knowing that the Creator wants us to succeed, we can now think positively.

Let's ask ourselves once more: Are we here for the gratification of our body alone? The body is destined to ultimately decay in the grave, so would the Creator create us with such a sophisticated spiritual and emotional apparatus if we were only meant to work like mules all of our lives, then die, and then become the equivalent of fertilizer in the soil? The body, with all that people invest in it – the spa, fancy food, workouts, massages, beauty treatments and whatever – ends up as ash. It's a harsh realization, but it's true.

The body is governed by physical gravity, which brings us down.

The soul is governed by spiritual gravity, which brings us up. So, the more we focus on our soul, the more we can think positively. The more we think positively, the more we succeed. Since the real "you" is the soul – and the body is merely its housing – you can certainly allow yourself to believe in yourself and to think positively. You can and will succeed!

Seven Reasons to Believe in Yourself

If you're still not convinced that you have every right to believe in yourself, here are seven good reasons why you can. Repeat them to yourself periodically until they become second nature:

1. **I am unique**. The Creator created me, as He did every other creature, with a unique

trait of my own that no one else has, just as my fingerprints are unique; there is no exception to this rule.

2. **I have a special job to do**. The Creator gave me particular attributes, skills and talents that enable me to accomplish my own very special mission on earth. If I'm not aware of my own special attributes, skills and talents, then I must find and identify them, for they certainly exist.

3. **I can accomplish my mission on earth**. The Creator gives each creation whatever it needs to perform its task. If a beaver can build a dam and a clam can produce a pearl, then I too can accomplish my mission on earth.

4. **The Creator loves me**. He is my Father in Heaven, and despite the fact that He has many children, He has no other child like me, for He created me unique in His own image. Since He is a loving Father in Heaven, He will always do what's best for me. This gives me confidence and all the more reason to believe in myself.

5. **I am a person of worth**. My soul is a

priceless tiny spark of Divine light. The more I enhance my soul, the more my worth is apparent.

6. **I have the power to improve myself.** Character strengthening and refinement are significant portions of every person's mission on earth. If the Creator gives us a job to do, He also gives us the power to succeed.

7. **I can be happy**. My happiness is not contingent on reaching the peak. I can be happy right now. Indeed, the happier I am, the greater my chances are of reaching the peak.

Repeat the above 7 reasons over and over, daily, until you internalize them. Once you believe in yourself, wait and see how your life soars higher.

In the coming chapters, we'll become better acquainted with our own special tools. This chapter has helped us to get to know ourselves and who we are. The coming chapter will help us determine where we are in life and where we're heading. Let's continue on our journey.

DAY TWO

DETERMINING WHERE YOU ARE AND WHERE YOU'RE GOING

A person with no goal or destination in life simply won't go anywhere. Many people just tread water, staying in the same place for years. But like water, when a person doesn't flow, he or she stagnates.

One word differentiates between a person who makes it up the mountain and someone else who stays at the bottom – desire.

Each one of us has had some situation in life where we've said to ourselves, "I must succeed". The stronger our desire, the more we saw what we were capable of doing. It doesn't have to be a life-and-death situation; it can be a football game or a race that we badly wanted to win. How many times do you see an athlete make a fantastic play in a championship game? You don't see such fabulous performances in practice games, because the player isn't playing with the same motivation.

Motivation and Desire

Motivation is desire, and desire is strength. When we're aware of our own strengths, we become so much more effective. So, in order to know where we're going, we must first know where we are. "Where we are" means that we recognize our strengths and our weaknesses. Once we do, even our weaknesses are an asset. For example, if a person is only 5'5" and weighs 130 pounds, then he probably won't succeed in reaching the NBA or the NFL as a professional basketball or football player. Yet, his lack of brawn will certainly not be a drawback in many other sports, such as long-distance running, judo or gymnastics. One's so-called "weaknesses" are not weaknesses at all, but merely navigational aids from Above to channel a person in the right direction.

A person is not limited by his or her so-called weaknesses. Lack of motivation and desire are what straps a person, not lack of intellectual or physical prowess. We'll soon see why.

Knowing who you are means also that you know where you are. We learned in the first chapter that the real "me" is the soul; desire comes from the soul, so one's desire is the most important indication of inner strength. Therefore, knowing where we are means that we honestly assess the levels of our desire and motivation. Then, we can accomplish anything we've set out to do. Without knowing where we are, we can't know which direction to take in order to reach the top of our personal mountain.

Suppose your destination is Kansas City, but you have no idea whether you're in New York, Los Angeles, Dallas or Minneapolis. Whereas a New Yorker must travel westward to reach Kansas City, someone from Los Angeles must travel eastward. A person from Dallas would have to go north, whereas his counterpart in Minneapolis would have to go south. Without knowing where you are, you can't possibly know which direction to pursue. No wonder so many people are totally lost in life.

As we see throughout this book, life is exactly like climbing a mountain; we begin at the bottom, and gradually work our way up in the direction of the "peak", our goals and aspirations. Without strong desire to achieve those goals and aspirations, a person goes nowhere.

Lack of desire and motivation leads to laziness and negative emotions. You'll never see a person with strong motivation who is sad and depressed. Therefore, the best teachers, coaches, commanders and employers are the ones who are capable of instilling desire and motivation in the hearts of those whom they are responsible for.

The various trails up different parts of the mountain resemble life's options – the daily choices a person must make that influence his or her entire future.

A hiker without a map, or with a map

written in a foreign language that he or she doesn't understand, can't possibly reach a destination. By the same token, people devoid of desire and motivation can't reach their destination either, because they lack direction, suffer needlessly, and never know which path to take in life. They're lost!

Living in this world without desire and motivation is like hiking up a mountain path on a moonless night without a flashlight. Imagine stepping in a crevice, incurring a serious injury, and then discovering that you had a flashlight in your backpack. What a shame! If you'd have known that you had a flashlight, you'd have safely navigated your way up the mountain.

The material world is analogous to a mountain. The course of our lives is a like the path to the top. Even though life is frequently "dark" with difficulties, our proverbial flashlight is our desire and motivation, which illuminate our way. Trying to get through life without the benefit of desire makes for an unbearable existence. Therefore, the key to living a physically and mentally healthful life, and a meaningful one as well, is having strong desire and motivation.

Life devoid of desire resembles a tourist who can't read a map or understand the language of the local directional signs – a lost soul in every sense of the word. It's truly frightening to think about the number of people who lack motivation, desire and direction in life, traveling down random roads and making major decisions in life by chance or instinct.

When an airplane flies through thick storm clouds, it feels constant turbulence. Flying is both difficult and dangerous, and the passengers – belted in their seats, jolted up and down and nauseated from the falling sensation in their stomach – have difficulty performing the simplest of tasks. Suddenly, the plane rises above the clouds to the clear blue sky and the shining sun. The passengers gaze out of the window and the gray mattress of cloudy turbulence is beneath them. The plane levels off at cruising speed and altitude, and the passengers feel calm and steady like they're sitting in their living room. They now resume their normal mode of functioning.

Motivation and desire take a person above the cloudy turbulence of basic survival in a non-congenial world. Without them, hardship is unbearable. With them, we weather the greatest challenges with strength and with a smile.

Not everyone has twenty-inch biceps, a 135 IQ or a beauty-queen face and figure. Yet, natural talent does not determine success. The underdogs who beat the odds are the ones with the strongest desire and motivation.

Natural talent is like an escalator. But motivation and desire are like running up a stairway, two stairs at a time. Even without the advantage of the escalator, the person who runs up the stairs will make it faster to the top. His life isn't as easy as the person riding the escalator, but ultimately, he's the one who succeeds.

How to Motivate Ourselves

Toward the end of the previous chapter, we learned that the Creator put us here on earth for a specific purpose, giving us our own special set of tools to accomplish our mission in life. The more we realize this fact, the more we're motivated to get to know our true selves and to put our individual talents and aptitudes to work.

If a person knew how important he or she was to the world, they'd be highly motivated. The more one realizes that every move he or she makes has a profound effect on creation in its entirety, the more they gain incentive to do their very best in all their endeavors.

Don't think that you are a simple individual. You're walking around with a spiritual microchip in your midst – a soul – which is a tiny spark of the Creator.

The intrinsic reason that many refer to Him as "Father in Heaven" is because He really is our Father. We all have the same spiritual DNA as He does, for our souls are tiny sparks of the Divine. This fact has profound implications. Just as He is unlimited, we are virtually unlimited as well. As we've seen with great people throughout history, human beings can accomplish virtually anything. Knowing that we are only limited by our desire is jet-fuel for motivation.

When we motivate ourselves to stretch

toward the stars, even if we don't reach them, we still ascend to great heights.

Choosing our Goal - Look at the Peak!

We can now move forward to pick the right destination - our goal in life.

Western society has duped people into looking for instant gratification, but that's usually cheap. You can't compare a cup of instant coffee to an aromatic demitasse of fresh stone-ground Turkish coffee that a Bedouin brews in the desert on an acacia-ember fire over the course of a half hour.

Two facts are axiomatic about things that come easily in life:

1. They're most certainly not our goal.

2. They won't take us to the top.

An Olympic gymnast won't get a gold medal by doing a somersault - any three-year old toddler can do that. The gymnast scores extra points by "level of difficulty" - the greater the challenge, the greater the reward.

Professional athletes suffer pain and

injuries. Why? Their rewards are commensurate with their dedication.

The path of least resistance is comfortable, but it won't get you to the top. Remember, "comfort" has nothing to do with gratification. Marathon runners do not live comfortable lives. But, they wouldn't sell their accomplishment of running 26 miles for all the tea in China.

Every individual on earth has an important task to do. The Creator does everything with an express purpose, so if He created a particular human being, it means that the world needs this person! With that in mind, don't ever sell yourself short. As we'll see in the coming chapter, each person has his or her own remarkable set of tools to perform their mission in life. Your mission in life is your own personal peak! You're not competing with anyone but your own negative inclinations.

Why the Difficulties?

When things come easy in life, we neither improve nor increase our desire and motivation. Life's difficulties, challenges and obstacles on the way to the top are designed to fuel our desire and motivation.

Even more, life's extreme difficulties force us to take stock in ourselves.

In engineering, there is a concept known as "tensile strength". Tensile strength measures the force required to push or pull something such as rope, wire, or a structural beam to the point where it breaks. The tensile strength of a material is therefore the maximum amount of pressure that it can be subjected to before total breakdown.

We can't know the strength of a material until we test it; in other words, until we expose it to extreme pressure and/or stress. In engineering, this is simply known as the "stress test". For example, a cardboard manufacturer frequently displays on the cardboard boxes he produces the amount of pressure that the box is capable of withstanding.

Our difficulties in life, when regarded with the above concept in mind, are all for our ultimate benefit, just as everything else the Creator does. Our "Manufacturer" wants to show us what we're capable of, which is usually much more than we think. Our difficulties in life are therefore none other than "stress tests" to show us our true emotional and spiritual "tensile strength." So, rather than protesting and complaining - which won't get us to the peak of our personal mountain - we'd be much better off strengthening ourselves emotionally and spiritually. Once we do, we are not only capable of reaching higher peaks, but our climbing in life becomes easier.

Let's come back to our original thought at the beginning of this chapter - where am I.

At age 33, I was "successful" according to my peers and the society I was part of. I had a good career in agriculture and in agri-products technology, was earning good money and had a wonderful social life. My two hobbies of long-distance running and art photography were both immensely enjoyable and prize-winning. Yet, I lacked the feeling of deep inner happiness and tranquility. I was restless and never satisfied.

When war broke out, my reserve unit was called up on active service. A subsequent face-to-face encounter with death showed me that I was on the wrong path in life. The most difficult day in my life became the best day in my life, because I started asking myself the real questions - who am I, where am I, and where am I going. Were it not for the near-death encounter, I might have been living a water-treading, superficial and meaningless existence to this day.

On that particular perilous day in the middle of a war, I decided to pursue a completely new path in life. Others thought I was daft, but for the first time in my life, I listened to the inner voice instead of the outer cackling all around me. That overhaul of my life was the best move I ever made until then; immensely gratifying, but certainly not easy. What's more, it wasn't the last of my overhauls, either. You can do it too if you follow your true aspirations with no fear.

Self-Assessment: Choosing the Right Goal

Don't be afraid to ask yourself some serious questions in life which most people avoid. That's why they're not happy!

1. What gives me the feeling of inner

gratification?

2. Do I have a goal or am I going nowhere?

3. Am I living according to my desires or according to the desires and expectations of others?

4. What are my good points?

5. Am I performing my task on earth?

By answering the above five questions, we will not only determine where we are in life, but we will be able to choose the goal - that particular path up the mountain - which will bring us to our personal peak.

From this moment on, forget about other people's peaks and paths. Keep focused on your own. Despite what society and the media tell you, you are competing with no one but yourself.

Let's elaborate on the above five questions; this will enable us to assess ourselves much more proficiently.

First, what gives me the feeling of inner gratification? Here, we must differentiate between the temporary thrill and lasting gratification. Sure, eating the chocolate-covered donut is heaven, but a sorely limited one. Most people regret eating it only seconds after they swallow the last bite, for all they're left with is the empty calories. With the proverbial "a minute on the lips but years on the hips," we see that not only the soul suffers anguish from the "instant joy" of bodily excess and indulgence, but the body itself pays the price at the expense of its own health and wellbeing.

We can therefore agree that eating chocolate-covered donuts - as well as other bodily indulgences - will not bring us lasting gratification.

What makes you feel good inside? What makes you proud of yourself? What gives you so much satisfaction that you don't need the praise or approval of others? The answers to these questions are markers that indicate the particular path in life you'd be happy and successful in choosing.

Second, do I have a goal or am I going nowhere? So many people in life are simply treading water, working to exist and existing to work. Is a bi-weekly or monthly pay-check all we have to look forward to? People are sad and depressed because they lack an ultimate goal. Hardship and pain are peripheral issues when a person is focused on a goal. But without a goal in life, one's frequent and inevitable challenges are unbearable.

There's a world of difference between an individual who practices medicine as a means to make money and an individual who dreams of easing human suffering. The former will never treat an inner-city child whose parents can't afford to pay; the latter - acting just like his Creator - has compassion on the sick child. By treating him, the merciful physician is making the world a better place.

Making money is a goal, but it's neither lasting nor gratifying. One of two things happen to money - either a person is taken away from his money or the money is taken away from the person. The two never remain together for posterity.

A meaningful goal is one that no one can ever take away from you.

A chinchilla exists, but it just keeps running

around and around on the same wheel. We are humans, not chinchillas. We can't go up the mountain until we get off the wheel that keeps us in one place, despite all the energy we're exerting.

Third, am I living according to my desires or according to the desires and expectations of others? So many parents often force children to do things that the child cannot stand. For example, the football-playing father who never made the first-string team dreams of his son being the star player and consequently forces football down his son's throat. But maybe the son dreams of being a violinist? Under his father's pressure, he'll never be happy or successful. He won't succeed as a football player and he won't be able to develop as a violinist. That's double frustration!

True self-assessment means taking a serious look at ourselves and asking ourselves probing, fib-busting questions, such as: am I doing what I want to do, or am I meandering along a path that others have made for me? Am I following the path that's right for *me*? What do I want from myself? Where do I want to go?

Am I properly utilizing my talents and strengths?

The answers to the above questions are additional markers that indicate the particular path in life you'd be happy and successful in choosing.

Fourth, what are my good points? Our good points are the special qualities, talents and aptitudes that the Creator instills within each of us. These good points enable us to climb our own individual mountain in life and reach our peak. They are our tools that facilitate getting us up the mountain. Just as a mountain climber needs a good back pack, ropes, boots, hammer, and pegs to get up the mountain, we need our own special tools to enable us to accomplish our mission in life, as we'll soon learn when we progress to Day Three.

Fifth, am I performing my task on earth? Positive answers to the previous four questions indicate that you're doing the job that the Creator sent you down here on earth to do. Here's why:

As we'll see in the coming chapter, the

Creator creates each and every being with unique traits of their own. **You are no exception.** The particular combination of attributes, skills, and talents that He instills in you enables you to accomplish your own very special mission on earth.

With the above thought in mind, if you feel unhappy or unfulfilled, you most certainly haven't yet tapped your own rich resources, and therefore are not yet putting them to work in fulfilling your own distinctive mission.

Don't be Fooled

Modern society dupes people into setting materialistic goals for themselves, but no money, fame or fancy "toys" can satisfy the soul. The soul is only satisfied when it fulfills its mission on earth. So, don't be fooled into making money or fame your goal in life.

Material amenities can't buy character improvement *or* inner peace, nor will they enable you to leave your mark on earth, unless your goal is to be a major philanthropist. The fame and fortune of Marilyn Monroe, Elvis Presley, Janis Joplin, Karen Carpenter, Jimmy

Hendricks and a long list of other rich and famous people didn't prevent their suicide and subsequent descent to the grave at an early age.

Finding my Destination

In this chapter, we've discussed where we are and where we're going. Once we take the candid answers of the five questions that we asked ourselves in self-assessment, and we add our personal prayers in our own words to the Creator to help us gain clarity, we'll surely establish the right destination to set our sights on. We become much more focused and productive, for we now have a clear goal. We no longer waste time on inconsequential endeavors. What fantastic blessings!

We have devoted Day Two to establishing where we are in life and where we want to go. We're now ready to identify and familiarize ourselves with our own special tools, which will help us climb successfully to our own personal peak.

DAY THREE

THE RIGHT TOOLS AND THE RIGHT PATH

Any experienced climber is extremely meticulous in preparing his or her backpack before a climb. The success or failure of an entire venture could depend on whether or not the climber packed a spare pair of shoelaces.

The Creator has already packed our backpacks for us. He has given us the tools we need to climb our own mountain and to reach the peak. Our job is to become acquainted with those tools, to refine and cultivate them and to utilize them properly.

Your Backpack

Your metaphorical "backpack" is your own unique set of talents and aptitudes that no one else on earth has. The Creator created you unique. You have your own special individual task to accomplish and mission to perform on this earth. Otherwise, you wouldn't be here. Nothing was created without a reason. Every creation is critical to the proper functioning of the universe.

King David couldn't understand why in the world the Creator created spiders. One day, alone in the desert, exhausted, his throat parched and limbs in agony, King David fled from his enemies[1]. The enemies pursued him mercilessly and were about to seize him.

King David had no choice – his last place of refuge was a cave. He crawled inside and cried out silently in prayer from the depths of his soul. He could hear his enemies approaching on horseback...

---

[1] See Samuel I, chapters 20 - 26.

A large spider began to weave its web on the opening of the cave. After a few short minutes, the entrance to the cave was completely covered by the spider web. The pursuers reached the cave. "He can't be inside there", they said. "Look at that spider web!" The spider saved King David's life, and King David no longer questioned the necessity of each and every creation.

If spiders are vital to the world, then how can you possibly think that you're not? As a human, you are the most magnificent creation!

Stop thinking that other people are better, smarter, or more talented than you. If you do think like that, it's a clear sign that you don't know yourself well enough. Either you haven't looked at all those wonderful tools in your backpack or you're unaware that they exist at all!

Jealousy is a Ridiculous Emotion

I'll prove to you how foolish jealousy is – it's a useless negative emotion that the evil inclination uses to disarm you, and it wastes a lot of your brain power, clarity and self-composure. Worst of all, it gets you down on yourself.

Have you ever seen a carpenter who's jealous of a plumber? Never! The carpenters are happy that they don't have to unclog drains and toilets like the plumbers do. Sure, the plumber has all types of monkey wrenches and tools that you won't find in the carpenter's toolbox. But, you don't need a monkey wrench to build a table. The carpenter is not jealous of the plumber, because he has his own job to do. Such tools as block planes, wood saws, lathes and nails are tools that no plumber will ever need.

And, if we look in the electrician's toolbox, we'll find tools that no plumber or carpenter has. He can replace a burnt fuse but he can't unplug a sink or build a table.

Once you know what your task is in the world, you'll never again be jealous of anyone. How do you know what your task is? Look again in your backpack. See what's inside. You'll find that even the tools you lack are helpful in helping you identify your mission in life and your best path to your peak. Do you realize what that means? Even your disadvantages are advantages! Let's see how:

If you're tone-deaf, your mission in life is definitely not to be an opera singer. And if you're severely near-sighted, it's not such a good idea to dream of being a fighter pilot. Why? You lack the tools. If you lack the tools, then that's not your task in life. Being tone-deaf or near-sighted will not hinder you if your dream is discovering a cure to cancer or teaching special-needs children how to read.

The Creator gives each person what he or she needs to do their job in life. Why be jealous that another person has a plow if he's a farmer and you're an accountant? Since when does an accountant need a plow? Maybe this example seems somewhat ridiculous, but when we look at envy and jealousy through spiritual eyes, they are truly ridiculous emotions.

Look at your good points. They're the tools in your backpack. Each is like a piece of a puzzle; put them all together, and you'll have a clear picture of what you're likely to succeed in. Once you piece together your good points, you'll see how the Creator is gently guiding along your own special path. Once you find it, you'll be heading straight for happiness and fulfillment. It's about time that you got to know your wonderful self.

Every person has his or her own "backpack" just like they have their own pair of shoes. Nobody thinks of borrowing someone else's shoes, for our shoes assume the individual contour of our feet. Even if someone else has the same shoe-size that we do, their shoes won't be comfortable if we wear them. That's why we are most comfortable when we carry our own backpack. Don't try to carry someone else's.

With the above in mind, don't ever compare yourself to others. Don't ask yourself all types of questions that rob you of your confidence, self-image and inner peace such as, "Why can't I be like John Doe? Why is Tony Ploni more successful than I am? Why is my sister-in-law so neat and organized," etc.? Ask yourself one question only: "What is the job that the Creator wants me to do?" When you find the answer, you'll be really happy.

Finding the Answer

The best and only way to truly find yourself and your special talents, as well as find your own unique path in life, is to set aside time for daily personal prayer.

The word "prayer" in English carries the connotation of supplication, making an appeal or a request as we do in our prescribed prayers. Yet in Hebrew, the word for prayer refers to an interaction with the Creator. Once we add the adjective "personal" to the Hebrew connotation of prayer, we get "personal prayer", which indicates each person's individual intimate interaction and communication with the Creator. Daily personal prayer is to the soul what daily nutrients are to the body.

As our own personal dialogue with the Creator, personal prayer reflects our feelings and mood at the particular time when we are engaged in it. The big added dividend of personal prayer is the insight we gain to ourselves as we share our most intimate thoughts with the Creator and verbalize them. This is a gift from a loving Father of Heaven who derives tremendous gratification whenever anyone of His sons and daughters speak to Him from the heart and seek to be close to Him.

Personal prayer is our daily chance to truly

express our individuality. Each person speaks to the Creator on a personal level. You don't need a house of worship or a particular prayer book. You speak in your native tongue personal jargon the same way you'd speak to a loving parent or caring best-friend. What's more, you don't need to belong to any particular religious group. As a unique child of the Creator, you have the inherent privilege of speaking to Him wherever and whenever you like.

Tell the Creator your deliberations and aspirations. He'll be happy to lead you along your own special path in life that's conducive to accomplishing your particular task on earth. Further advice from an upright life-coach facilitates this as well, as we'll see in the continuation of this chapter.

The words of personal prayer aren't written anywhere except on the walls of an individual's heart. There is no greater manifestation of one's individuality. Personal prayers are the ones that are readily accepted because they're said with intent and true sincerity.

There's an additional beautiful aspect to

personal prayer. Suppose you set aside time for your daily intimate meeting with the Creator and the words don't come – you're suddenly tongue-tied and don't know what to say. No problem! Express yourself by way of your guitar, flute, piano, violin or whatever instrument you play. If you don't play a musical instrument, sing a song that inspires you. You'll soon feel a warmth in your heart that will melt the obstruction that's preventing you from speaking; the words will soon flow forth. So as you can see, the path of personal prayer is not the beaten path of the masses; it carves your own invigorating trail up the mountain.

Not only does personal prayer differ from person to person, but it changes from day to day. We strive to be in constant growth, both spiritually and emotionally. We aren't the same people who we were yesterday. Not only that, but the world around us has changed since yesterday. Each day brings new circumstances, new challenges and sometimes new goals. We should also monitor ourselves daily to check if we're on the right path. Personal prayer helps us clarify things and assess ourselves, keeping us on that right path. For that reason, daily personal prayer is so very important.

Lesson of the Railroad Track

One's mission in life can be compared to a railroad track. A person who is doing the right thing is "on track" while someone who is off on a tangent, either wasting time or dabbling in matters of no consequence is "off track."

The train from New York to Washington has its own special track. If somehow it began moving southward on the track that's intended for the use of the northbound Atlanta-to-Boston train, there would be a disaster. In like manner, as soon as any of us attempt to traverse a path in life that's not our own, we not only fail to reach our own destination and attain our own goal, but we certainly don't succeed in fulfilling the other person's mission. In short, when we're off track we either get totally lost or suffer all types of collisions in life – emotional, spiritual, and even physical. This is yet another reason not to envy or compare ourselves with any other person on earth.

We should certainly refrain from the gross unfairness of comparing our spouses to other people's spouses, comparing our children to other people's children, or even comparing our children to each other. Such comparisons are destructive. Parents must remember that just as each of them has an individual mission on earth, each of their children has individual missions on earth. Comparisons to others are therefore cruel, unfair and counter-productive.

Don't ever try to "jump track" and pursue someone else's path. As we noted earlier, if a person was born with weak eyesight, then he wasn't meant to fly an F16; being a fighter pilot is not his mission in life, so why be jealous of a person with 20/20 vision? Several world-famous musicians were blind or crippled; their physical handicaps did not hinder them in the least from pursuing their mission in life.

In light of the above, don't ever lose heart because of what you think is a lack of talent and dexterity. And, don't have pipe-dreams of being someone else. Focus on your own unique talents and aptitudes without comparing yourself to any other person on earth. Direct your energies to doing the best with the tools you **now** have at your disposal in your own backpack, and you'll surely succeed!

Don't Be Discouraged

The right path is seldom the easy path, so don't be discouraged from the difficulties along the way.

In a successful army, every soldier has a training path designed to enable him to perform his future tasks. For example, merely teaching a pilot how to fly a plane is not sufficient. To be a good pilot, he must also learn physical fitness, navigation, aerodynamics, meteorology, weapons ordinance, and parachuting, just to name a few. A pilot trainee doesn't complain when he's sent to cope on his own for seven days in the desert, for he knows that survival training could save his life in the future. He doesn't become sad and depressed when he has to navigate on foot through difficult terrain, complaining, "Hey, I'm a pilot; what do I need these ground exercises for?" He knows that everything along his training path is designed for his ultimate success and benefit.

By the same token, the Creator tailors a unique path in life for each of us, giving us experiences that we will need to do our jobs and utilize our talents. Every trial, tribulation, and ordeal is just another stepping stone to strengthen us and to help us reach our goal successfully. Knowing that everything in our lives is part of the tailor-made path in life that the Creator maps out for each of us, there's no room at all for sadness or despair. We never get lost, and we always find our way. That means that we have direction in life; we therefore become much more efficient in doing whatever we do.

Break Out of the Bottle!

A person asks himself: "Why don't I make it to the peak? Why don't I ever make upward progress?"

So many people seem to be standing still or treading water at best. For them, simply staying afloat is an accomplishment.

Who wants a life of simply staying afloat? I don't know many people like that. Everyone wants to reach the top, but so few do. Why?

Folks are trapped in a bottle. They exert

themselves, they hustle and they might even make a lot of noise in the process, but they don't go anywhere. Why? They're just running around inside the bottle…

When you were in your formative years, all types of people put labels on you. Better yet, they put labels on a bottle and stuck you inside. As a young person, you subconsciously thought that your parents, teachers and peers knew what they were talking about. So, when you were trapped inside a bottle labeled "dumb", "cowardly", "lazy", "ugly", "uncoordinated" or "failure", then you thought that you were dumb, cowardly, lazy, uncoordinated or a failure.

Because you were trapped in a bottle, you never tried out for the school play. Why? When you were seven, your mom asked you to take out the trash and you forgot. She called you "stupid" and said that your memory is terrible. You surmised that if you can't remember a small task, how can you learn and remember an entire script? Maybe you wanted to learn karate but you never did, because when you were nine, you backed down from fighting an eleven-year-old bully who was much bigger than you and your dad called you a "coward".

Because you were trapped in a bottle, you never really succeeded in school. Whenever you didn't feel like doing the dishes or washing the floor, your mother called you "lazy". When you worked your hardest trying to pass a math test that few in your class did well on, and you came home with a 70, your father said you were "dumb".

And when the class queen or the class king snubbed you, you really felt worthless.

That's a thing of the past. Now that we've decided to reach the peak and we've learned that we have the tools to do so, we will now rid our brains of all those false labels that confine us and restrict us, holding us back from succeeding.

Obviously, one can't grow or climb a mountain if he or she is trapped in a bottle. Even worse, the longer a person is trapped in a bottle, the more he assumes the shape of the bottle, just as a plant's roots assume the shape of the pot that it grows in. But in a bottle, there's no room to grow.

We therefore must break out of the bottle -immediately - in order to start growing.

Suppose someone called you a coward. I'll prove to you that you're not a coward. Think of something you believe in with all your heart. This might be some ideal that makes your life worth living. You'd go to great lengths to defend that ideal. That's courage. It's right there within you, but you can't feel it inside the bottle.

Suppose someone says that you're ugly. They're blind. The Creator creates each creation with its own intrinsic beauty. But you won't be able to see your own beauty if you're trapped in a bottle. Bottles distort images.

Conforming to peers is the worst type of bottle. Your peers won't let you grow. They certainly don't want you to reach the peak, either.

The core truth is that the Creator designs each of us in a way that we can best perform our task on earth. A tractor isn't jealous of a Ferrari's leather upholstery and a Ferrari certainly isn't jealous of the tractor's big tires. Why? Each has its own task to perform. Sure, the Ferrari is prettier than the tractor, but it can't plow a field.

Breaking out of the bottle means that we do some good, cogent self-assessment, evaluating our strengths and weaknesses. The more we get to know ourselves, the less we're prone to be trapped in a bottle. Once we're out of the bottle, we can really start climbing.

The Life-Guide

Behind every winning athlete is a winning coach.

Even the best reconnaissance soldiers make use of local scouts when navigating their way through foreign or strange terrain. Relying on someone who can successfully guide them through the dangers and pitfalls of an unfamiliar area can be a life-saver that prevents costly mistakes.

Some people use the term, "spiritual guide" while other say, "life-coach." I like the term, "life-guide", a synthesis of the two. Complementing our self-assessment and personal prayer, an upright and objective life-guide is not only a great sounding board for our ideas, but he or she can prevent us from making costly and needless mistakes, including spiritual and emotional vertigo.

Vertigo is a term that jet pilots use to describe spatial disorientation. When a pilot approaches the sound barrier, strange things can occur, especially on a clear-day's flight over water. The pilot is liable to become disoriented, and to confuse the blue of the sea as the blue of the sky, and vice versa. Some pilots become dizzy and others elated; in any event, vertigo causes disorientation whereby the pilot thinks that up is down and down is up.

Today, jet pilots undergo rigid training to prevent vertigo. They learn to trust their avionics - those sophisticated flight instruments that show a pilot the course, speed, altitude, and position of the airplane's axis in relation to the earth, including a screen that displays an artificial horizon - and not to trust their own judgment. That way, a pilot can know whether he's "up" or "down". A pilot's unshaken belief in his instrument panel is therefore vital to his survival.

People experience a lot of emotional vertigo, and oftentimes don't know whether they're up or down. They stubbornly trust their own judgment, and therefore make serious mistakes in life that take years to repair. Some mistakes are like prison cells that incarcerate them, so they need someone with a "key" who can let them go free. That's where a life-guide comes in.

A trusty, knowledgeable, and upright life-guide can keep anyone on an even keel and on a path of success. If you don't as yet have a life-guide, keep your eyes open for an individual of intelligence, modesty, wisdom, faith, impeccable character and selflessness. If you have access to such a person and trust his or her judgment, then latch on to them! Chances are that you've found the right life-guide for you.

This world is very confusing. A person can become completely disoriented in this world - literally insane - without a life guide, following all types of paths that lead to misfortune, disillusionment and outright danger. That's what causes spiritual vertigo.

If you're flying a jet aircraft, keep one eye

on the control panel at all times and you'll avoid vertigo. If you're navigating your way through life, keep an eye and ear open to your life-guide, and you too will avoid the type of spiritual disorientation that could cause a crash-landing or lead you on the wrong path in life.

Finding Yourself and Your Path in Life

Let's summarize this chapter with a few pragmatic pointers that will help us find ourselves and our path in life.

Never forget that the Creator creates each and every being with a unique trait of its own. You are no exception. The particular attributes, skills, and talents that He instills in you enable you to accomplish your own very special mission on earth. Even your apparent disadvantages are advantages, designed to channel you towards the right path to your own personal peak.

If you're unhappy with your lot in life, you most certainly haven't yet tapped your own rich resources, and therefore are not yet fulfilling your own distinctive mission. So don't put the blame on others. Go for your dream! If you have the talent to develop a cure for cancer, you won't be happy as a cashier in a drugstore. If the Creator gave you a brilliant mind, you're wasting your potential wallowing in front of a television screen.

Wait and see how your life improves once you start cultivating your own special abilities. You'll be a lot happier with yourself, and at peace with the world around you. Others will like you much more as well.

Until you've found those special qualities or talents of yours that set you above and apart from everyone else, you haven't yet started to live a truly satisfying life.

The Creator outfits every human with at least one outstanding quality in a raw state waiting to be developed, like a muddy unpolished diamond deep inside a South African diamond mine. Yet, unlike the South African mine, you don't have to travel to the far corners of the world to discover *you*. By implementing the advice of this book, you can start right now.

The Personal Assessment Chart

For your convenience, here's a personal assessment chart for you to fill in. It will help you become much better acquainted with yourself, and it's a great tool to find your path in life. Use it like this:

1. Look for your good points in the "talents" column; list your particularly special attributes, skills, or talents. These are the ones that you should be cultivating to the best of your ability.

2. Divide your weak points into two categories: First, those you have control of; and second, those you don't have control of.

Talents	Faults we can control	Faults we can't control

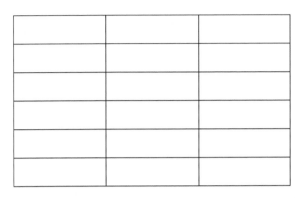

Let's follow this simple path to self-improvement: do what you can to focus on improving the weaknesses you can control while being careful not to confuse uncontrollable faults with the controllable faults you can overcome with dedication and hard work. Don't forget that the uncontrollable faults are not really faults at all, but road-markers to show you which paths in life are not yours.

Most importantly, take maximum advantage of your strengths, and be sure that you're putting them to work.

The path the enables you to best use your talents is your path to the peak. We're ready to start climbing.

DAY FOUR

THE CLIMB - FOCUSING ON THE GOAL

Now that we know who we are, we know where we are. Then, we decide where we want to go, identify our path and begin our actual climb. As we climb, we'll realize how essential our pre-climb preparations are.

Everything we do in life is like climbing a mountain. We start at the bottom and work our way to the top. Maybe you know people who start near the top, for they were born in circumstances that granted them special advantages - but don't be jealous of them. Over the long run, those who started at the bottom and worked their way up are the ones with solid character and true gratification. Everyone respects a self-made individual, but few have regard for the person who was born with the proverbial silver spoon in his or her mouth.

At the bottom of the mountain, our view is limited. The higher we climb, the more breathtaking the view. Yet, our enjoyment has a price-tag to it. We humans have an ingrained trait, namely, that we don't fully appreciate anything unless we work for it. Therefore, we won't find an easy path that takes us to the top, no matter what our goal or destination is. But the climb – striving to attain the objective we've focused on – is the spice of life. It strengthens us and builds our character. The satisfaction of achievement that results from exerted effort is something that money cannot buy.

Modern society has fooled people into thinking that easy is good. Advertising that wants us to buy instant this and instant that tries to brainwash people into seeking instant gratification; they've succeeded tremendously. An entire generation's health is suffering because they've been accustomed to manufactured microwave meals and fast foods. Many young people don't know what slicing a tomato or shredding a head of lettuce is.

Suppose that hi-tech found a way to build an elevator to the top of Mount Rainier. Reaching its peak would no longer be an accomplishment. But not only that – by reaching the top of a mountain in an elevator, one doesn't earn the title of "climber". He or she neither strengthens their character nor earns true gratification.

The higher we climb and the steeper we climb, the more we exert ourselves. Our calves and quadriceps are singing a song of strain. No matter the shape we're in, our muscles groan. Our lungs burn. Yet we keep climbing, even when our body says, "enough!"

What gives us the strength?

When the body kicks out, desire kicks in. There's not a single long-distance runner or mountain climber that reaches a peak or finish-line on physical prowess alone. As such, the ones with the greatest desire often surpass those with superior physical ability. This rule applies not only to climbing, but to any endeavor in life. Keep it in mind and you'll reach your own unique peak in life.

Real Progress

The dubious mate of instant gratification is instant progress. The old adage says, "Easy come, easy go." If your ascent to the peak is easy, something is therefore wrong.

Czechoslovakian folklore has an anti-hero called Shveyk. He's the simpleton that does everything wrong. Shveyk gets sent off to the battlefield to engage the enemy. In a short time, he returns to his home base. "I'm victorious," Shveyk declares. "I captured Hill 131 single-handedly!"

"You imbecile!" yells the commander. "Hill 131 was already in our hands. The soldiers you shot were our own troops!"

No worthwhile victory in life is easy. Climbing is both strenuous and tedious. True upward gain is step-by-step and inch-by-inch. True progress – whether in athletics, academics, career or spirituality – is gradual and measured.

Suppose a person played all semester long, and then a week before final exams, he or she starts cramming, staying up all night. If they're dexterous enough, they'll pass their exams. But, they won't know the material. The laws of memory retention teach us that the more we learn and review, the more we retain. As such, true learning takes time.

The same thing goes for body-building. A person can do a strenuous workout and get the blood pumping to his biceps and triceps, and for a short time, he'll look like Mister America. But less than an hour later, he's back to his flabby self. What's worse, if he tries to lift too much too fast, he'll pull muscles and suffer injuries. So as with learning, proper physical conditioning needs to be slow and steady. One doesn't become physically fit overnight.

Take your time on the climb to wherever you're going. Remember Aesop's fable about the tortoise and the hare. The people who make the rabbit-speed progress are usually flashes in the pan. Those who make a slow and steady climb eventually reach the top. In the course of a lifetime, it doesn't matter if you've achieved your goal a year earlier; what matters is that you climb steadily and ultimately reach the peak.

Meanwhile, until we reach the peak, we might be having all types of pains, difficulties and obstacles. But as we go higher, the view just gets more and more exhilarating. The climb is well worth it.

Let's keep in mind four important points during our climb:

1. Life is short - we have no time to waste on peripheral or inconsequential matters; in other words, those things that have nothing to do with reaching our goal.

2. Keep focused - many things try to sidetrack us, so we don't want to wake up some morning and find ourselves in the complete wrong direction.

3. Don't let the pain discourage you - every gain comes with pain; the suffering strengthens character. There is no such thing as a painless ascent to the peak.

4. Don't let other people discourage you - be courageous and honest with yourself and strive for your goal undaunted.

Let's elaborate:

Life is Short - Don't Waste Time!

People who strive toward their goals are happy people. Happy people easily connect to the Creator. The Evil Inclination doesn't want you to be happy, because it certainly doesn't want you to connect with the Creator. Therefore, it does everything in its power to prevent you from attaining your goal, as we'll see in the following parable based on the teachings of the 18th-Century spiritual healer Rebbe Nachman of Breslev.

Imagine this scene: It's mid-morning on holiday-eve in a busy outdoor marketplace, where everyone is feverishly preparing for the fast-approaching holiday.

More than a dozen women are clamoring around the fishmonger, each trying to purchase a fresh carp for the holiday. The fishmonger and his helper can barely manage while trying to clean and scale the fresh fish and deal with all the yelling ladies prodding them to hurry up. Right in the middle of the holiday-eve mid-morning chaos, some stranger runs by the fish stand and waves a tightly closed fist, as if he has the Hope Diamond in his clasp. He yells out to everyone, "Hey, nobody knows what I have in my hand - and nobody will know, because I won't show you!" He then runs away.

The fishmonger's helper throws down his knife and runs outside, chasing the stranger. "Hey Mister, stop! You gotta show me what you have!" The ladies are curious too, so they start running after the fishmonger's helper. The poor fishmonger, in desperation, chases his helper and the ladies. What bedlam! He doesn't know who paid and who didn't, and whose fish he was cleaning; and the holiday is only a few hours away...

The stranger runs by the butcher's stall. There, about twenty or so ladies are waiting in line while the butcher's helper plucks feathers from freshly-slaughtered chickens. What a sight! Chickens squawking, feathers flying, and two dozen ladies arguing about who's next in line. The butcher is trying valiantly to accommodate everyone by cutting up their chickens like they each requested, while his knife flies a lot faster than any eye can follow. Now, amidst all the holiday-eve butcher-shop pandemonium, the stranger yells out to everyone, "Hey, nobody knows what I have in my hand - and nobody will know, because I won't show you!" He then escapes the butcher's stall into the market's main street.

With a half-feathered, limp and lifeless chicken in hand, the butcher's helper leaves his festival-eve battle station, runs out into the street in hot pursuit of the stranger, and shouts, "Hey Mister, wait a minute! You gotta show me what you have!" The chicken-purchasing ladies are curious too, so they run after the butcher's helper.

What a hullabaloo! The stranger, now being chased by the fishmonger's helper, the butcher's helper, more than fifty screaming ladies with children, dogs and cats joining the crowd, looks over his shoulder and teases the crowd with a sly guffaw, "You'll never find out what I have in my hand!"

Soon, the greengrocers and their customers, the dry-goods merchants and their customers, the peddlers, the bakers, the candle-makers and almost everyone else in the area are all chasing after the stranger. The whole village of more than a thousand people gasp for breath trying to catch up with the swift-footed stranger.

When the stranger looks over his shoulder once more, he smiles a familiar self-satisfied, sadistic and sinister smile. He has done his job superbly; not a single individual in the marketplace remembers what he or she should be doing - preparing for the holiday. No one remembers that there are only five short hours left to bake bread and biscuits, cook fish and chicken and clean house before the onset of the holiday at sundown. The market is emptied and unattended. The townspeople are in an uproar.

Unexpectedly, the stranger stops in his tracks, turns around and faces the crowd. "Now, I can show you what's in my hand!" He opens his fist and showed them an empty hand. "The joke's on you, you foolish nincompoops!" Gloating over a job well done, he disappears into thin air...

* * * * *

You can probably identify the stranger in

Rebbe Nachman's tale, the one who caused all the chaos: he was none other than the Evil Inclination! He's still in our midst, convincing us that he has something valuable in his empty hand. He's still trying to sidetrack us from pursuing our main mission in life while tempting us to waste our time chasing things of absolutely no consequence.

Today, the Evil Inclination's intellectually-devastating and spiritually-empty hand holds social media websites, chat rooms, web forums, news websites, computer games and many more and even worse distractions that waste your time and leave you empty-handed.

Ask yourself how much time you spend aimlessly surfing on the web, bouncing around from link to link like a little metal ball in a pinball machine. An hour? 45 minutes if you're really time thrifty? More? How many hours a day are your eyes glued to your smartphone, WhatsApp, incoming messages and emails? Even if you don't yet suffer from kyphosis and destroyed posture, you're not accomplishing a fraction of what you want or need to do every day. The time just seems to slip through your fingers...

A person can walk more than five kilometers (well over three miles) in the same hour that he or she wastes surfing aimlessly on the web. Not only would they be doing a favor for their heart, lungs and entire body, but they'd be burning about 350 calories. That means that in twenty days, they'd lose 1 kg (2.2 pounds) without changing their eating habits or dieting. Within 6 months of walking instead of web-surfing for an hour a day, they'd lose a whopping 9 kg, which is nearly 20 pounds. They'd look great and feel great. But what do they gain after six months of Facebook, Twitter, and chat rooms? Nothing!

Let's stop running after the empty-handed fool right now. We can if we want to.

Focus is our best weapon against distraction.

Focusing on Our Goal: Breaking Bricks

Did you ever wonder how a little 105-pound Korean Karate specialist can break a whole stack of bricks? Our friend "Kim Wong" is intensely focused on his goal. He is thinking of nothing else. His powers of concentration are immense. Nothing else is on his mind at the moment. Not only that, he's optimistic and goal-oriented. He has been training and preparing for years. He didn't learn this skill by watching a You-Tube movie yesterday.

Stick Kim Wong's hand in an x-ray machine, and you'll find that his bones are larger and denser than normal. This is the result of his year after year, day by day intense training and no-nonsense diet.

Without Kim Wong's "perfect strike", the result of his long-term goal setting, his desire, self-discipline and deeply intense concentration, he'd shatter his hand and wrist on the first attempt at cracking a brick.

There's a lot to learn from Kim Wong's brick breaking.

If you want to reach your peak, don't fret about yesterday and don't worry about tomorrow. Yesterday is gone and tomorrow isn't here yet. Those who fret about the past and worry about the future aren't focused on the present. As such, they are not effective and they certainly don't succeed.

Climbing, like any other endeavor, requires intense concentration on whatever we're doing right now. Lack of attention and focus not only retards success but could be outright dangerous. Focus is therefore the secret of success both in material and spiritual endeavors.

Your focus on the task at hand, your concentration, dedication and goal orientation can make you exemplary even in the world of brick breakers.

Let's look at "Richard"; he'll likely remind you of someone you know:

As a tenth grader, Richard said to himself, "Why work hard?" He walked around with an MP3 in his ear, spent hours of text-messaging with his friends every day and ate junk food. Although he had an excellent math teacher, he day-dreamed his way through class. "No sweat," he told himself, "I know enough to get into the local community college; I'll apply myself there when the time comes."

Community College turned out to be a

bigger bore for Richard. He'd text-message his way through classes, and say, "Big deal - college is not the real world. I know enough to pass exams and get a degree. I'll buckle down when I start my career..."

Somehow, Richard made it through community college by Google Search and cutting-and-pasting his term papers. He'd play all semester then copy people's review summaries and cram for a few nights before finals. In fact, his college didn't require learning; only memorization. Richard decided that he'd start hustling once he hit the real world of employment.

Not really qualified for anything, Richard took whatever job he could find. He was never happy; he was always thinking that the next place of employment would be better. There and then, he'd get to work...

Richard's apathy, laziness, and lack of focus made his young wife go crazy. She couldn't contain herself, so she yelled at him all day long. The marriage lasted for five months.

Richard's second wife was his perfect

match, just as procrastinating and lethargic as he was. She spent all day on Facebook. On Wednesday night, the dishes from last Sunday would still be in the sink. Candy bar wrappers were all over the floor, together with the empty Coke battles.

Today, Richard is already pipe-dreaming that his third wife will keep a neater house...

Richard couldn't break a brick in a million years. He's a loser, right? Who does he remind you of?

How many people say, "The heck with tomorrow; let me enjoy myself now!" Anything that's inconsequential doesn't last. And anything that doesn't last isn't true enjoyment. There is no enjoyment like climbing - striving for our goal, because our achievements are truly lasting. No one can rob you of the immense gratification of performing your task and reaching your personal peak.

The Pain and the Gain

Before we speak about pain, an integral part of any climb, let's reinforce our desire to reach the top, for desire enables us to overcome the pain. We've spoken about desire in previous chapters, but we need to reemphasize the importance of desire; it's our prime asset and main tool in reaching the top.

Desire is a gift from Above. Desire fuels our spiritual and emotional engines, motivates us and gives us the power to make a difficult climb to the peak in life that is our destination.

Imagine that you're standing in a beautiful valley, at the base of a mountain. You've heard from people who have reached the top of the mountain how breath-taking the view is from up there. You also know the difficulties that others have had on the way up. But, the weather is gorgeous, you gaze once more at the peak, and you long to be there. The greater the desire, the more you feel surges of energy in your calves and quadriceps. Your body and your soul both seem to be telling you, "Get going! Start climbing – you can do it..."

Since this world is the world of free choice, every force is coupled with an opposite force. Good and evil are pitted against one another, what we've referred to previously as the evil inclination and the good inclination. Force must overcome gravity, not only on a physical level but on a spiritual level as well. Desire, too, has its nemesis - obstacles.

Whenever we want to do something really important, especially in the process of achieving one of our lifelong goals, we encounter obstacles. This is a stark spiritual fact that's inherent in creation. The more that our goal is critical in performing our mission on earth, the greater the obstacles.

Many people with the modern instant-gratification or path-of-least-resistance mentality say, "Hey, that's not fair! Why do things get in my way?" Sir Isaac Newton gave us the answer – for every action, there is an equal and opposite reaction. Therefore, where there is no desire, there are no obstacles. Where the desire is tremendous, so are the obstacles.

Who would pay $1000 for a ticket to the Super Bowl, to the World Series, or to the NBA finals if there were only one team on the field or court? No one! We all enjoy seeing the heroic champions overcome the stiff opposition in earning their victory.

Here's something important to remember when life becomes especially difficult: tradition teaches that when an individual is struggling to overcome obstacles in performing his mission on earth, the Creator Himself and a Heavenly stadium-full of angels are rooting for him or her to succeed.

With the above thought in mind, looking at the world through spiritual eyes is always encouraging. One who does so sees that obstacles are a gift. Obstacles fuel desire. Especially when it comes to climbing our own personal peak in life, the greater the obstacles, the more we desire to reach our goal. We see this in everyday life: put a lollipop in a toddler's hands, and before he has a chance to remove the wrapping, grab it back. The toddler will most likely wail and start running after you to grab the lollipop. Before he encountered the obstacle – the adult who took away his lollypop – he may have desired it. But now having encountered the obstacle, he desires the lollipop so much more.

People who become disheartened from an obstacle lack desire in the first place. Becoming discouraged from doing something merely means that you don't want it that much.

Pain is one of life's greatest obstacles and an integral part of personal growth.

Have you ever noticed how champion athletes endure pain and injuries on the way to achieving their goal? No professional football player wins a Super Bowl ring without having been hit really hard, repeatedly. A professional athlete will pay virtually any price to reach his peak of achievement, the national or world championship.

I have never seen a special-forces soldier with an obstacle-free life. In administrative units, life gets a lot easier after basic training. Not so in combat units. The more elite a unit is, the more its troops suffer difficulties and obstacles daily, with virtually no let-up. How and why are they prepared to do this? The more they believe in their mission, the more they are willing to do anything to accomplish what they have to do. If they don't believe in their mission, they'll suffer tremendously, both physically and emotionally.

The relationship between believing in your mission and success is important in every phase of life, not just in the realm of athletics or the military. The more a salesman believes in his, product, the more successful he or she will be. The more teachers believe in what they teach, the more successful they will be in instilling those teachings in their students' minds and hearts.

Let's return to our own personal mountain and continue climbing. We have our goal – the peak. We have our tools – the wonderful individual talents and aptitudes that the Creator has given us to fulfill our mission in life, our personal peak. We have our path up the mountain – we know what we need to do to reach the peak. The better we've prepared ourselves, the more proficiently we are now climbing.

We're now on the way up, step after step. Our initial climb is exhilarating – the grade is not so steep and every step upwards reveals a better and more beautiful view.

Gradually, as we progress upwards, several things start to happen. No matter how well-conditioned we are, our breathing becomes more difficult. The grade gets progressively steeper and each step demands more energy. We reach a point where both our lungs and the muscles in our legs feel like they're burning. We feel the pain of the climb. It's not easy. The innocent looking peak, when seen from below, now looks so much more challenging.

With the air becoming thinner at the higher altitude, breathing becomes even more difficult. Maybe we've never learned anatomy, but we now become familiar with each individual muscle in our legs, for each one is crying out in pain.

Do we give up? For sure, not! Two things encourage us – another glance at the peak and the gorgeous view below. We never dreamed how beautiful the world could be, and the higher we go toward our goal, the more beautiful the world gets. This is not just a metaphor, but a fact of life.

The more we truly desire to reach our goal, the more we'll be able to overcome any obstacle. So don't say that you can't reach your peak because there are obstacles along the way –

that's no excuse. When we truly desire to achieve something and believe in our goals, leg pains, lung pains or any other obstacle won't stand in our way. The gain is well worth the pain.

Keep climbing, and don't ever be discouraged. Our desires invoke obstacles, but the obstacles fuel our desires. Remember that always, and you'll make it to the top of your own personal peak. Pain is a part of the gain.

Let's summarize what we've learned until now.

When climbing, focus on your objective and don't get sidetracked. Don't waste time and don't let pain discourage you. Remind yourself of your goal. When things get difficult, remind yourself of why you set out on the path to your peak in the first place and reaffirm your faith in what you're doing. This will give you a shot of encouragement and the strength to keep on going.

Be True to Yourself

The biggest liar is one who lies to himself.

In Shakespeare's Hamlet, Polonius says to his son Laertes, "But above all, my son, to thine own self be true."

When a person lies to himself, and he tries to be someone else or something he's not, he becomes a double loser: first, he can't possibly be the other person, because he doesn't have the tools that the Creator gave to that other person. Don't forget that other people have their own special, completely different missions on earth and therefore different tools. Second, he's not himself, and he's not using his own special tools to accomplish his own designated task on this earth.

Many people who speak to me often tell me that they're embarrassed of their true inner aspirations.

That's a tragedy. You'll never find a mountain-climber who's embarrassed to be climbing his mountain.

Your dreams, goals, and inner aspirations are your spice of life. The more you believe in them, the more they give you the power to fly out of bed in the morning. What do you care what other people think? Do they care if you're happy or not? Don't bet on it.

Henry David Thoreau said, "If a man does not keep pace with his companions, perhaps it is because he hears a different drummer. Let him step to the music which he hears, however measured or far away." How did Thoreau come to this amazing conclusion? He spent hours on end in solitude. He came to the conclusion that the Creator dwells not only in all of creation, but in every person's soul.

What does it matter if people turn their noses up at your melody? Flow with your own melody and step to the beat of your own drum, for that's exactly what the Creator wants from you.

Above all, be straight with yourself.

The folks who'd rather be Facebooking or watching TV don't understand climbers and achievers. Don't let them or anyone else to discourage you!

Keep in mind these five points, which will always help you on your climb in life:

There is a sure-fire way to become great,

but it's not an easy path. The five steps to greatness are as follows:

1. On your climb, be prepared to sacrifice comforts and personal amenities. The goal is well worth it.

2. Be prepared to march courageously along a different path than your peers are taking.

3. Be prepared to suffer disparagement and humiliation. Few people understand true climbers in life and look at them as if they are weird or eccentric. But don't worry - the climbers have the last laugh; even if they don't reach the top, they end up on a higher level than everyone else.

4. Shun conformist attitudes of mediocre masses.

5. Finally, tenaciously pursue the truth. It will always lead you on the right path.

Let's move on to Day 5 and learn how to cope with difficulties and setbacks that we invariably encounter along our path to our own personal peak.

DAY FIVE

DEALING WITH DIFFICULTIES AND SETBACKS

Today, we'll learn how to cope with difficulties and setbacks. Just as there are rocks and boulders on a mountain, there are setbacks and difficulties on every path to any of life's peaks. To get to the top, we must learn how to deal with them.

Although the Evil Inclination attempts to convince people otherwise, periodic falls are part of growth. More often than not, a fall indicates that a person is ascending. If one hasn't climbed anywhere, there's nowhere to fall.

For your happiness and self-preservation, I

want you to engrave the following rule of life on your heart and mind:

As we go higher up the ladder of personal growth, our setbacks of today are actually *higher* than our successes of yesterday.

Let me explain: Suppose that four months ago, you never gave much thought about your dietary lifestyle. But since, you've done some routine blood tests; your doctor warned that your cholesterol is a bit high. Full of motivation to improve your overall health and physique, you've started an extremely healthy diet, eating only vegan, raw, unprocessed foods.

After a few weeks of adjusting your culinary tastes to your new eating habits, you're starting to watch the pounds melt off and have noticed a dramatic improvement in your energy level. Everything is great, until one night your friends treated you to a birthday dinner at the best steakhouse in town. After having allowed yourself to indulge in a few high-calorie drinks, you decide to skip the grilled salmon/salad combo and opt for a perfectly seared, richly marbled Delmonico steak, and end the night indulging in a creamy, fluffy chocolate soufflé.

The next morning, you're really beating yourself up over your major slip-up. Instead of focusing on all of the months you've followed your diet without fail, you decide to focus all of your attention on last night's feast. Here's what you should remember, though: even though you've taken a fall, you're still miles ahead of where you were four months ago.

Plugging in your actual fall to the above example, know that whatever you've taken upon yourself to do or to improve on, there will be falls from time to time.

So, since we're human, and we all fall periodically, we must learn how to take a fall without getting hurt. The first thing a good gymnastics instructor teaches students is how to take a fall. A paratrooper spends days learning how to fall before he ever goes up in a plane. And the first thing that a pilot learns is how to take an aircraft out of a downward spin. An experienced investments broker must know how to redirect investments when the stock, bond, or commodities markets fall. And, what holds true in the physical world holds true in the metaphysical world. If we must be prepared for a physical fall, we should certainly know how to handle an emotional or spiritual fall.

Basically, we're all babies, especially when compared to our potential. Babies can't possibly learn how to walk without falling occasionally. But, remembering the benefits of a fall is the best cushion for a fall.

Let's examine the five good reasons why we sometimes fall or fail:

1. Only doers fall. If you don't climb mountains, you don't fall on the rocks - simple as that! People who drive sometimes get traffic tickets. People who don't drive never make wrong turns. Wouldn't it be ridiculous if a seventy-year-old person bragged that he never committed a traffic violation if he never drove a car? The first consolation of a fall is the knowledge that you are a doer and a climber.

2. A fall teaches, and not only triggers a stronger second effort but reveals untapped potential. Periodic falls safeguard us against complacency and arrogance. When we fall, we realize that we need to try harder the next time. Frequently, a second effort is far superior to even a best first effort and reveals additional untapped potential that we didn't even know that we had. So, if you fall, don't be disappointed; just "get back in the game". If you pick yourself up, then your fall is only a temporary setback. What's more, it's usually a springboard to greater achievement. Don't forget, as long as you're alive, the game's not over!

3. Failure brings us closer to the Creator. If we were constantly successful, we'd probably walk around with our noses in the air. Then, we'd be ugly, heaven forbid, because few things are uglier than arrogance. The Creator wants His children close to Him. After a setback, we pray a lot harder and earnestly seek Divine assistance for our next effort. If our lives were a perfect string of non-stop successes, we certainly wouldn't pray from the bottom of our hearts.

4. Experience is life's best teacher. The experience of a fall drives a lesson home immediately. Usually, we are slow in internalizing and implementing what we learn. When we fall, we have a golden opportunity to better ourselves immediately; we quickly learn the lasting lessons of a fall and deeply internalize them.

5. Small-scale failure assures large-scale success. Where would an actor prefer to forget a line - in rehearsal or on stage? A failure in rehearsal often assures a better performance on stage, since the actor makes a special effort to polish the rough edges of his or her performance. Frequently, small failures are none other than preparations for large successes.

The fear of failure, like other fears, paralyzes people. Once we shed our fear of failure, we can "un-paralyze", and initiate a new and better effort. My old high school coach taught me a cardinal principle in wrestling that equally applies to any situation in life: "You don't lose the match by being thrown to the mat; the faster you're back on your feet, the better your chances of winning!"

What Happens if I Fall?

Go ahead and ask yourself, "What happens if I fall?" Don't be afraid; be prepared! If you were to fall off a horse, your riding instructor would tell you three things:

a. Pick yourself up.

b. Dust yourself off.

c. Get back on the horse and make a new start.

Who can improve on the above advice? So, you've fallen into a relapse of anger? Big deal! How many times have you succeeded in overcoming anger lately? No, you haven't lost everything. Make a new start. New beginnings are spiritually and physically beneficial to your life. Try making the following declaration:

On the long run, does it matter if I didn't succeed? No, it does not! From this moment on, I simply declare a new beginning! The past does not concern me! I'm about to make a fresh start doing the best I can.

Declaring a new beginning is tantamount to spiritual rebirth. How? The spirit influences the body. So, when the spirit declares a fresh start, the body becomes rejuvenated! By removing our focus from setbacks and disappointments, we avoid sadness and depression. By declaring a new start, we reenergize and empower ourselves. The cheerfulness of a fresh emotional and spiritual start keeps our face, body, and complexion looking younger than any spa or cosmetics will. A fresh start is *the* secret of staying young.

Let's take a day-to-day example. Suppose we're caught off guard, and we lose our temper with someone close to us. Spiritually, we've been knocked down, but the game's not over. If we suck in our pride, give our loved one a thoughtful little gift and a sincere apology, we turn our setback into a major victory. We rejuvenate ourselves, and our relationships with others. A fresh start keeps us happy, youthful, and optimistic. We have a great day and we keep on climbing!

Better than Ability

Sooner or later, during any climb or endeavor, ability and strength kick out. The true test of a person's caliber is how he or she acts and reacts when there's simply no more reserves of strength and ability to draw on.

Do they give up? Many do. The few who reach the peak don't. That's the entire difference between the masses and the select few. The select few never give up.

I don't remember a single soldier in the elite combat unit that I was privileged to serve in that had a worse physique than I did. Many marveled at the fact that I succeeded in qualifying for the unit. Virtually all my comrades had better ability than I did. But I had a greater measure of one important quality than anyone else - perseverance. I never gave up. This was both on a physical and a mental level.

During the most grueling maneuvers, I'd hum to myself the old Ringo Starr hit from back then, "It Don't Come Easy." I'd fire myself up and keep going. Rambo-types who could chew me up in a bar fight were falling to their knees. I was still on my feet and moving forward...

My life is a living example of how native intellect, strength and ability don't determine your success; desire and faith do.

On a mental level, whenever logic says that there is no solution, tell yourself, "True; maybe I don't have a solution, but the Creator in His infinite wisdom surely does. Father in Heaven, please illuminate my brain and show me the way." This leads to out-of-the-box thinking that helps you to circumvent obstacles. This is also the product of an unwillingness to give up – your desire and your faith.

Desire and faith give you the strength to persevere. Perseverance gets you to the top. And what's more, it has saved lives on plenty of occasions.

Under a deadly onslaught of enemy fire, the infantry platoon inched forward toward their objective. One soldier screamed, "I'm hit! Oh, my G-d, look at my arm!" A bullet had fractured his right elbow. He was bleeding badly and the pain was excruciating. He dropped his rifle to the ground, and his good left arm embraced his right elbow. Close to panic, he continued screaming, "My arm! My arm! Someone, help me!" His buddies in the meanwhile were pinned down, trying to return fire and stay alive. The wounded soldier was no longer shooting back. He was vulnerable. Before long, a second bullet struck him – in the head.

One of the other soldiers in the platoon was also badly wounded in the right arm, but no one knew. A nasty enemy bullet tore his entire bicep open like a grapefruit; he felt like daggers of fire were stabbing him over and over in the arm. Never had he experienced such torturous pain in his life. But he gritted his teeth and didn't say a world. With his good left hand, he slipped another clip into his carbine and kept on shooting. He and his comrades mumbled a silent prayer and then took the biggest gamble of their lives: with their weapons blazing, they rushed the enemy position and overcame the enemy forces. He lived to tell the story.

Both soldiers in the above incident were severely wounded. But the difference between the dead soldier and the surviving soldier is resilience: one was overwhelmed at his setback whereas the other found a way to persevere, bounce back and continue fighting.

* * * *

Ron was a photographer for a leading travel magazine. He was climbing in the Austrian Alps on an exquisitely beautiful cloudless late-spring afternoon. He was excited, for he had captured some of his finest photos that day. Reaching a ledge with a breathtaking panorama, he set up a tripod and began taking photos of the setting sun. Totally engrossed in what he was doing, Ron didn't feel how rapidly the temperatures were falling. He knew that hundreds of thousands of people would be seeing the internationally-circulated magazine featuring these photos, both on the cover and in the feature article, so nothing else mattered at the moment.

From out of nowhere, the gust of a strong Alpine wind blew across the mountain, spraying wisps of snow and ice, mountaintop remnants from the last snows of spring. Reeling from the gust, Ron's tripod suddenly stood on one leg — in another split second, his camera with all the day's photos would be plunging thousands of feet to the canyon below. Ron lunged for the tripod and succeeded to prevent it from falling, but the rock he stepped on in doing so didn't provide a firm footing. He lost his balance and fell off the ledge. In one moment, he saw his entire life flash before his eyes. Soon, he'd no longer be alive...

Ron's free-fall was short-lived. Another ledge, seven feet below the ledge he was standing on, protruded enough to catch the photographer and save his life. But with his feet in the air, he landed with a pounding thud on his right side, his ribs and shoulder absorbing the bulk of the blow. The fall was so hard that Ron's lungs completely deflated. He gasped for air, but there was none. His ribs screamed in pain – at least two were broken. His shoulder was dislocated. His legs and arms were scraped and bleeding and he had a gash on his forehead. Yet, he was alive. Two problems remained: he still couldn't breathe and his backpack and cell phone were on the upper ledge. So were the camera and tripod, which he had succeeded is saving from oblivion.

Ron's initial reaction was despair. "Show's over!" he thought. "If I don't choke soon, I'll freeze. How can I ever make it back up to the upper ledge? I can barely move..."

Then his resolve kicked in. Ron was never a quitter and his tenacity more than compensated for his lack of natural ability in other areas. Determined to beat the odds but knowing that he couldn't do it on his own, Ron pleaded in his thoughts, "Dear G-d, I can't go on much longer without breathing. I need Your help..."

After a seemingly endless period of fifteen or twenty seconds, his lungs somehow inhaled a cold but ever-so-sweet live-giving breath of Alpine air. The temperature was now in the high thirties and all Ron was wearing was a sweatshirt. Soon, it would be pitch black, for the sun had set. This was the last chance to find a way back to the upper ledge, where the lifeline of the backpack and cell phone was. Ron pictured the future magazine cover in his mind's eye. He wasn't ready to die on the rocks. With a superhuman effort, he pulled himself up to safety.

Ron's ribs never healed properly. Neither has his shoulder. But his photos continue to grace the covers of magazines and inspire people. What's more, he continues to do great things.

* * * *

Success doesn't mean that you never fall; it

means that you're perseverant and resilient - you never give up and you make every effort to get back on your feet as quickly as possible after a fall.

People dream of an easy life. In reality, there is no such thing. Anything of worth in life worth requires effort and effort is an upward battle, just like climbing a mountain. The Creator designed the world in such a way that everything of substance falls – that's the law of gravity. So, in ascending, we must go against the forces of nature, which seldom cooperate, to say the least.

Pondering the concept of gravity could be potentially depressing. True, if all we are is a physical body, then we will be pulled downward.

Fortunately, as we learned in Chapter One, we are not merely a physical body. Our bodies serve as the housing for our life force, the soul. The soul also functions according to the Creator's laws of creation, but unlike the body, the soul pulls us up. Determination, resilience, tenacity, perseverance and faith - all qualities of champions - come from the soul. So, if we want to be champions in whatever we do, we must strengthen our souls and learn to get back on our feet after a fall, for falls are an unavoidable part of life. We don't want them, but once they're here, we can take advantage of them in our striving for success.

The Afterburner

The great thing about perseverance and never giving up is that anyone can acquire these wonderful traits. Since they are the most important in reaching your personal peak, then anyone can reach the top.

Few of us are born with 135 IQs. Not everyone is born with natural bodily coordination. Some people are much slower learners than others. And, some people are naturally disadvantaged, having been born with handicaps.

Yet, anyone can build a strong desire. Anyone can learn to persevere. That means that anyone - including you - can reach the top.

When strength and ability kick out, desire and perseverance kick in.

Desire and perseverance become

supercharged when you engage a certain afterburner - faith.

Faith means three things:

1. There is a Creator who not only created the world but runs it and sustains every single creation from the greatest galaxies to the smallest one-celled organisms, which of course includes every single one of us with no exceptions.

2. Everything the Creator does, whether we understand how or not, is intrinsically good and for our ultimate benefit.

3. Everything the Creator does is for a specific purpose. The events in our lives and the stimuli of our environment are His way of communicating with us.

Let's suppose that we're climbing the mountain, or we're in any other situation that is challenging, beyond our strength and ability to cope. What do we do - surrender? No, giving up is not part of our lexicon anymore. But we've run out of strength and we have no more gas in our tank of ability and potential. We kick in the afterburner - faith.

We said that when strength and ability kick out, desire and perseverance kick in. So now, let's suppose that we're physically and emotionally exhausted, and even our desire and perseverance are at their rope's end. Then what do we do?

Remember what we just learned? Slow down and internalize this life-saving golden rule: **Desire and perseverance become supercharged when you engage your afterburner of faith.** Maybe we've run out of physical and emotional gas, but the Creator is unlimited and all-powerful. He's there to help us; all we have to do is to turn to Him.

It's that simple.

Do you need help? No problem - just speak to the Creator in your own words. You don't need a house of worship or a clergyman. The Creator is right there with you 24/7, ready and willing to answer your call for help.

Here's a big secret: many, if not all of our difficulties in life are designed to bring us to the conclusion that we need the Creator's help. The more we cultivate an intimate personal relationship with Him, the more readily we witness Divine intervention and assistance in our lives. Life's waters are too treacherous to try and navigate them on our own.

A Complete Turnaround

Faith enables us to use the momentum of setbacks and difficulties to turn our lives around for the very best. Here's how:

Understanding that a given situation of a setback or difficulty is for the best is not *believing* that it's for the best. From a spiritual standpoint, comprehension is a much lower level than faith. At the point where the brain no longer understands how the Creator is doing everything for the very best, faith begins. In other words, faith kicks in when the brain kicks out – that's why we call it the "afterburner".

In trying times, whenever the brain complains that a certain situation is bad, we can do ourselves a tremendous favor by putting our brains aside and activating our faith in the Creator; namely, that everything is from Him, for the very best and for a purpose. If we listen to our brain, then the game's over – we've lost.

When logic despairs of finding a solution or overcoming a difficulty, those who depend on logic are all raising the white flag. Do you know what that means?

Winners and achievers are much less rational and logical than losers.

Notice the sports pages of the Monday-morning newspapers; you'll usually find interviews with the coach of the losing team, who has all types of rational excuses and explanations of why his team lost. But why do they rarely interview the winning coach?

Winners don't have to give excuses and explanations of how and why they won. In fact, most winners can't fully explain why they won, for the reason frequently defies logic.

How does faith help us succeed in the bleakest of situations?

With faith, we don't succumb to negative emotions. We don't tell ourselves how tremendous our problems are, we tell our problems how tremendous and infinite the Creator is - He can do whatever He wants whenever He wants. Faith gives us optimism, and when we're optimistic, our brains operate much more efficiently. Therefore, faith actually enhances our brain power and our ability to cope under any situation.

Faith illuminates our hearts with the confidence that the Creator has a good reason for everything He does, and the currently rocky roads will eventually lead to smooth and peaceful paths. By letting our faith override the logic of our brains, we can readily rise to any challenge which life throws our way. Faith is therefore the best way out of any difficulty.

DAY SIX

SELF-RENEWAL - THE SECOND EFFORT

The previous chapter gave us a new outlook on coping with setbacks and difficulties.

An optimistic attitude is an integral part of reaching the top. Few do so on their first effort. Winners and achievers are the ones who persevere.

As a little boy growing up in the USA, my favorite cartoon character was Charley Brown of "Peanuts", the perennial lovable loser. Charley Brown's creator, Charles Schultz (1922-2000), was probably the most popular and influential comics author and illustrator who ever lived. Yet before he tasted success, he too was a lovable loser. He failed every subject in the eighth grade. He flunked physics in high school, getting a grade of zero. He also flunked Latin, algebra and English. And his record in sports wasn't any better. Though he did manage to make the school's golf team, he promptly lost the only important match of the season.

Charles Schultz then decided to pursue a career in drawing, having been proud of his artwork. His high-school yearbook editors rejected the work he submitted. He still believed in himself. So, after high school, he submitted a portfolio to Walt Disney Studios. They rejected him too. Charles Schultz didn't give up. He decided to tell his own life's story in a cartoon where the main character would be a little boy who exemplified the chronic loser who millions of people would learn to identify with and love, a global star, "Charlie Brown."

Jenson Button is a British race-car driver who won the Formula-One World Championship in 2009. Yet, he flunked his first driving test at the age of 17.

Sir Edmund Hillary participated in two

abortive attempts to climb Mount Everest before he succeeded on his third attempt in 1953.

Benjamin Cardozo, renowned Justice of the United States Supreme Court and former Judge of the New York Court of Appeals, failed at his first attempt at the New York Bar Exam.

Schultz, Button, Hillary and Cardozo - like many other winners - were the ones who kept reaching for the top even when they failed to reach the top. In fact, every step that they made toward the top was a success in itself.

In the previous chapter, we learned that there are good reasons - for our own benefit - why we have failures and setbacks in life. In addition, the Creator has some excellent reasons for not letting us succeed on the first try.

Many people ask a seemingly tough question: if the Creator controls everything, and He loves me, then why doesn't He let me succeed?

We'll preface our answer by noting that falling short of our goals is definitely a type of tribulation, since our lives are much more pleasant when we taste success. But the tribulation of interim failure is like a cloud with a silver lining. With that in mind, here's why the Creator often withholds initial success:

1. The Creator delays success until we can properly learn to nullify our egos, so that the success won't lead to arrogance, for arrogant people forfeit their connection with Him.

2. The Creator often delays success to encourage us to make a second, more concerted effort.

3. Delayed success is a test of faith.

By accepting our interim circumstance with optimism, we show that we are worthy of future success.

The Alternate Path

One additional reason that we don't succeed in reaching the peak that we set our sights on is that we might be climbing the wrong mountain or ascending the wrong path.

Life's difficulties and setbacks frequently necessitate a reevaluation of where we're going in life.

Sir Isaac Newton was tasked with running his family's farm after his father died, but he failed miserably. If he'd have succeeded, he'd have never attended Cambridge to study physics.

Walt Disney worked for a Kansas City newspaper as an illustrator but was fired for "lack of creativity."

Steven Spielberg started producing movies only after he'd been rejected admission to the University of California for the third time.

Having studied agriculture in university, I used to be a farmer, raising tree-fruit and turkeys on my mountaintop farm. At the age of 33, a skirmish with death while on active reserve duty in the military triggered my comprehensive reassessment of where I was and where my life was going. I decided to become a clergyman, spiritual guide and life coach and virtually started all over again.

Nearly nine years down my new path of theological studies, ordination and internship took me in the direction I wanted to go, but my peak was still in the distance. During the next twenty years, I had significant accomplishments: I had my own radio show on Israel National Radio; the books I authored were successful but the ones I translated became smash international bestsellers. I was the English-language editor and columnist of an internationally-acclaimed web portal and lectured frequently around the world. Yet, something was still missing. I was much too involved doing what others demanded from me and not doing what I really wanted to do. This was taking its toll on my body and on my soul.

Meanwhile, I was witnessing how fitness of body and soul are dependent on each other. Those who came to me with spiritual and emotional difficulties often had physical difficulties – many of them self-induced – that I couldn't ignore. Yet, I lacked the needed expertise to help them, and felt an inner voice tell me, "Do something about it! You have the capability of acquiring the tools you lack. Go for it!"

At age 62, once more, I began to pursue a brand-new path of learning new skills that included studies in anatomy, physiology, biomechanics, the science of fitness training, nutrition and preventative medicine. Five years later, by age 67, I had earned certifications in fitness training, health coaching and nutrition. As the rabbi and spiritual guide that I already was, I could now look at health in a truly holistic fashion that takes both body and soul into account. I retired from all my other activities to pursue my true desire of helping others enhance their spiritual and physical health simultaneously in my own unique way. The satisfaction has been indescribable.

No, it's not happy-ever-after, but it's all good. During an overambitious day of kettlebell training and wind sprints, the apex of which I ran 100 meters in 1.6 seconds less than the world record for my age group, my heart went berserk. My heart monitor's alarm buzzer was calling my attention to the urgent fact that my pulse had hit a terrifying 220! I was subsequently hospitalized with atrial fibrillation ("Afib"). Nothing the doctors did could bring heart back to its normal rhythm.

This new health challenge required me to

fine-tune the way I eat and exercise. With the help of my wonderful cardiologist Dr. Gideon Paul, I am able to live a full-throttle life that believe it or not, includes wind sprints and kettlebells, although on a somewhat less vigorous scale. The Almighty was teaching me a vital lesson that I have been able to pass on to many others: take care of your body, but don't make it your objective. Its task is to house and serve the soul.

Looking back, were it not for my all my setbacks and traumas, I would never have found the very best path to my own special peak.

Don't ever let setbacks disappoint you. Someday, you'll look back and realize that they were all for the best and necessary stepping stones along your way. Keep reaching. This is the goal of our sixth day - we keep reaching with a renewed second effort, and sooner or later, we'll reach the top. We don't allow anyone to discourage us. As long as we believe in ourselves and in our goals, and we keep reaching, we're in effect at the top already. Every step we make toward the top is success in itself.

Keep Reaching

Did you ever wonder why babies reach for things constantly? Is it their curiosity? Not really. A baby's reaching is indicative of our inborn aspirations to go higher, to achieve. The Creator instills strong hopes and aspirations within us, for they serve as the prime tool in helping us realize our potential, perform our mission on earth and accomplish great things.

Frequently, negative influences stifle our will to continue reaching. Negative comments from parents, teachers and peers gnaw away at a person's self-image and belief in himself. Unsuccessful efforts and a modern-day inclination toward laziness and instant gratification lead too many people to throw up their hands in despair, when in truth, they have every right to continue striving and to reach upward in hope.

Anything that stifles your aspirations in any way, or anything that discourages you from reaching as high as you possibly can is none other than an agent of the Evil Inclination, the source of all negativity. Aspirations and depression are mutually exclusive. As long as you have aspirations and faith, no one or nothing can discourage you. A discouraged and depressed individual is far from the Creator, just where the Evil Inclination wants him or her to be.

Because of their difficulties in life, people think that the Creator has forsaken them. Nothing could be further from the truth. More than anyone, the Creator wants you to succeed. I'll prove it simply, as follows:

The Creator created the world in order to reveal His majesty and monarchy. Such natural wonders as Niagara Falls, the Matterhorn, or a peacock's feathers certainly attest to Divine majesty. The greater the kingdom, the greater the king. With this in mind, would a world full of ugliness, losers and incompetents add to the Creator's dignity? Certainly not! Not only is it in His best interests that every one of us is happy and successful, but He created the world so that we could have every blessing and success. The more the world and its inhabitants are healthy, wealthy, wise and fulfilled, the greater the Creator's prestige! He wants us all to be successful.

So why aren't we?

The answer is simple - either we don't reach high enough or we've stopped reaching altogether.

Many people have attained milestone achievements in life, yet fade back into unhappiness, depression and obscurity. Why? They've stopped reaching.

Even if we've reached the peak of Mount Everest, we mustn't stop reaching. As long as we are still here on earth, there's more to be done.

So, if the Creator wants us to have every single blessing of success, then why do we still have deficiencies in life? Again, all of His blessings are hovering over our heads this very moment. We simply must reach for them.

How do we reach?

We pray. In our own words, we ask the Creator for whatever we desire. Each word of prayer creates a suitable receptacle for Divine abundance. If a moment of prayer creates an 8-

ounce receptacle, then an hour of prayer creates a one-hundred-gallon vat.

We wouldn't pour fine wine on the floor. In like manner, the Creator does not bestow blessings of abundance, both material and spiritual, unless a person prepares a suitable receptacle - prayer!

Aspirations without prayer are like trying to climb a mountain without taking the first step. But, aspirations with prayer will get us to our personal peak every time, as long as we never give up. And, in time, we'll conquer progressively higher peaks. Looking back, we'll find that today's reality is the product of yesterday's prayers and dreams.

Maybe you know people who have "succeeded" without prayer. That's not true success. Anything we obtain without prayer is ultimately detrimental, like all the people who went crazy from becoming millionaires overnight after winning the lottery. Success without prayer breeds arrogance, and arrogance leads to anger, dissatisfaction and a host of additional negative emotions that negate happiness. That's not success.

Success that results from prayer enables a person to feel the Creator's love. This leads to genuine happiness and inner peace. Just as no one can prevent us from praying, no one can prevent us from pursuing true happiness.

Since our souls are tiny sparks of Divine light and the very essence of the Creator, we share His attributes. Just as He is unlimited, so is our potential. And, in order to enhance and maximize our potential, we must reach for the stars. Even if we don't land up there between The Big Dipper and Orion, we'll still land pretty high, provided that we never stop reaching.

People that reach fly out of bed in the morning. They look forward to a new day and they're not afraid of challenges. They don't expect things to come easy, so they don't fall apart when they encounter obstacles. They are so accustomed to reaching that they jump over the hurdles that stand in their way.

As long as you continue reaching, rest assured that you'll reach your own personal peak. Once you get there, you'll see additional peaks that you never dreamed of. Keep reaching, and you'll reach them too.

Conclusion: Those Who Do and Those Who Don't

Let's summarize some of the key ideas we've learned in our six-day path to the peak, so that we can carry them with us wherever we go. Be sure to review this book from time to time, until its principles become second nature:

Those who don't reach the peak fail once and stop reaching. Those who reach the peak fail a hundred times and continue reaching until they eventually succeed.

Those who don't reach the peak are trying to be like someone else. Those who reach the peak are trying to be themselves.

Those who don't reach the peak think that success is only at the top. Those who reach the peak experience success with every tiny bit of progress along the way.

Those who don't reach the peak work for material goals. Those who reach the peak work to make themselves and the world a better place.

Those who don't reach the peak see "illogical" things they don't understand and become disheartened. Those who reach the peak see things they don't understand, put their logic aside, trust the Creator and get recharged.

Those who don't reach the peak attempt to conquer the world all at once. Those who reach the peak add up all their individual tiny successes.

Those who don't reach the peak focus on obstacles. Those who reach the peak look past the obstacles.

Those who don't reach the peak want to get ahead of others. Those who reach the peak don't harbor anger and jealousy, so they're happy to help others get ahead too.

Those who don't reach the peak follow society's definitions of success. Those who reach the peak follow their own soul's definition of success.

Those who don't reach the peak escape fears. Those who reach the peak deal with fear, face-to-face.

Those who don't reach the peak waste time

in inconsequential endeavors such as TV, social media and web-surfing. Those who reach the peak never waste a moment and are constantly building body, mind and soul.

Those who don't reach the peak are sad and depressed. Those who reach the peak are happy with whatever they have at the moment, even though they're constantly striving to improve.

Those who don't reach the peak look down. Those who reach the peak look up.

Don't forget, cherished friend, you're never alone. I believe in you and you have every right to believe in yourself. Godspeed, and may your journey to the top be filled with every blessing and all your heart's wishes for the very best, amen!

Join us at

"Strength and Serenity"

www.brodyhealth.com

Made in the USA
Middletown, DE
12 April 2022

64089348R00077